Remember, Recapture, Reclaim, Restore, and Preserve: Principles for Living

by

Stephanie Brendlyn Coursey Bailey

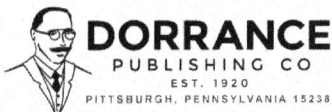

DORRANCE PUBLISHING CO
EST. 1920
PITTSBURGH, PENNSYLVANIA 15238

Dorrance Publishing Co
585 Alpha Drive
Suite 103
Pittsburgh, PA 15238
Visit our website at *www.dorrancebookstore.com*

ISBN: 978-1-6376-4128-6
ESIBN: 978-1-6376-4767-7

In the throes of the worst,
what other story could be told
which can remind us of the better?

This is a reflective companion to the documentary *Through My Father's Eye*, co-produced by the Author and Rob Hubbard of Bamboo Doors Studios. Nashville, Tennessee.

Written with a hint of a novel, but more like a narrative nonfiction, this treasure goes from my father's story to mine, intertwined with history, GOD and America to emphasize the thread of thoughts. Following my thoughts to their natural conclusion(s) had me ending up where I was surprised at times. Quotes from the grands, the siblings, or those who have viewed the documentary, interrupt the narrative flow—not distractingly but to accentuate the story's essence. Each chapter has a twist, poses a question, causes a realization and can relate to the reader on some level. Don't miss the double meaning of some phrases or words—both meanings being significant unlike your usual double entendre.

I dedicate, with appreciation, this book—which came about because of my documentary (Through My Father's Eye)—to my parents, James Robert Coursey, Senior and Willie Mae McClure Coursey. Through them I was allowed to see so far. With pleasure, this creative document allows the generational stories to be passed forward to my beautiful grandchildren and the generations of children seeded by my siblings.

I am grateful for the volumes of books and their authors that have attended to my love for reading. A varied assortment of them presented wisdom for this book.

I am grateful to and acknowledge JESUS CHRIST, my LORD and SAVIOR, for many nights of words, phrases, topics and encouragements that came to me and filled the pages that are presented to you in this book. My cup does runneth over.

FOREWORD

When Dr. Stephanie Bailey asked if I would like to review her book, I was pleasantly surprised. I expected to read a wonderful rendition of her childhood that might be similar to my own, or even very different. Being somewhat the same age and both in the healthcare field, though she a doctor and me a nurse, I knew there would be common themes. I read the book knowing that only God could bring us to the same place in our beliefs and worldviews. Dr. Bailey has brilliantly shared with us how she arrived where she is now, how her past shaped her, and how her God directs her. In sharing her vulnerabilities with us, she also poses questions that, if allowed, the reader will begin to ponder their own worldview and wonder where adjustments need to be made. That, my friend, is God's work, if you will allow Him. Is Dr. Bailey always right? No, but God is.

I planned to read it slowly and share my thoughts. What I found myself doing is reading from start to finish despite my own life challenges in the Pandemic of 2020. I would read late at night and then start again in the morning. I was captivated, and you will be too. How did the 60s and all of the racial challenges that we were faced with cause a young girl to ponder her beginnings and also ponder her creator, knowing that His life plan for her would be the best? How can we take those same questions that Dr. Bailey asked herself and turn them inward to reflect on our own feelings and beliefs? How can we challenge ourselves to consider our changing world, rise above the voice of chaos, and seek the voice of God's truths? We do that by reading, reflecting, praying, and then considering where we are wrong and what do we need to change. Do we even know that we have a worldview that directs our paths? Dr. Bailey challenges the reader to reflect on these questions. I had to make myself go to bed because I wanted to finish reading in one setting. It is that captivating. I have devoured it and am so honored to read this book.

Dr. Bailey's father's simple recordings on his Bell and Howell camera show a time in American history where there was unrest. In addition, there were families, communities, and family values that challenged us as racial tension was all around us. We all remember those times, but Through My Father's Eye *causes us to think about our childhood experiences again. Interestingly, both Dr. Bailey's father and my father could see from only one eye due to injuries. My father lost his eye in World War II, and Dr. Bailey's father lost his eye playing baseball. These losses changed their lives but did not destroy them. Mr. Coursey reminds us of a time when our world was changing. What did we do right, and what was wrong during that time in our lives? How can we make changes for our children and grandchildren? I believe Dr. Bailey's hopes are in the book. It makes me think of my childhood and also how I can make things different for my grandchildren.

If you will take the time to read the pages and listen to the documentary, it will probably take you by surprise on how twisted untruths can subtly take hold unless we are aware. This is what Through My Father's Eye *will inspire in the reader. What can we do differently to make things better for our children? Dr. Bailey takes us back to the dining room table and the stories shared in that setting. I shared her story with my grandchildren, who were six at the time, at our own dining table. The twins listened to me as I talked about Mr. Coursey and how he would walk to school while the bus driver passed him with the "privileged" children who rode to school. One twin said, "That is wrong," and the other said, "That is history." They then started thinking about themselves and talking about how they are different and how they are working through those differences in their childlike understanding. That is what Dr. Bailey will inspire you to consider. You will also realize that there are many subtleties in today's culture that are tricking us. I challenge you to take the time to read the book and ponder the many questions at the end of each chapter. It is not a quick read. If you will come back to the dining *table and sit down to think, you can help assure that your future is navigable and not directed by a twisted worldview.*

Dr. Bailey also talks about life in the 60s and her front porch, where much of Denton life passed by her house daily. We don't do that anymore, but we should seek other ways to slow down and grasp life as it passes by. I drove by someone rocking on her front porch recently. She smiled and waved. I smiled and waved. It is time to find a way to go back and discover where life has become too fast to ponder and learn.

This documentary and book are masterpieces. In this world where being privileged is seen as a weakness, realize that you too are privileged as a child of our creator, God.

Judy Goforth Parker, Ph.D., APRN

CONTENTS

I CALLED HIM "POP."

[Sometime during my late teens or early twenties, I decided to call my "Daddy" "Pop"...nothing much more about that decision.]

He always worked hard. He dropped out of school in the ninth grade to work full time [ten to fifteen cents an hour; $11.00 per week] and help support the family. At age fourteen, he established his first business—a shoeshine stand—which he built himself outside of the neighborhood store. He charged ten cents for a shine. A good day would net him about $1.50. The year was 1938. At age seventeen, he lost his right eye while playing baseball. His career dream was to be a mechanical engineer; he went to volunteer for the military—he had not been drafted—and was told he was ineligible to volunteer because of the loss of his right eye. He wished he could have gone on the spaceship *Sputnik* because of his interest in space. He always wished he could have finished school.

Pop arose each morning at 5:00 A.M. and was out of the door by six. I fixed his lunch each evening for that next day of work. I remember fixing bologna, souse—both bought at 5 cents a slice from Truxon's store down the street; peanut butter and jelly; leftover meatloaf or whatever meat was available from dinner the night before; and Spam for his lunches. He would return each night with an empty pail. At eight years old, what a show of appreciation! Did he really eat the lunch I had prepared? I'll never know, but I know my dad well enough to know he probably did.

While working one day on a strainer underneath an oil truck at Callis and Thompson (C&T) in 1963, some gas leaked on to his sleeve.

> *"The hot air from the exhaust caught his sleeve on fire. The creeper he was on got stuck as he tried to roll it out. He rolled off of the creeper to get out and more gas got on his back and burst into flames. Struggling in a shocked panic, he managed to get out from under the truck before it exploded. Other workers put the fire out – his glasses had melted on his face."[1]*

He suffered third-degree burns over 70% of his body. I was 13 years old and to this day the song "Soldier Boy" by the Shirelles evokes vivid memories of that time in our lives. It came on the car radio every day during the 32 miles of Mom's drive to take us to visit our father at the hospital in Milford, Delaware. We had to peer through a screened-off room to see him wrapped in bandages from head to toe—only a hoarse voice letting us know it was him. He was hospitalized 98 days. He recovered and resumed his work eventually, not bitter, not wanting to sue, nor be a victim. He was blessed, and he knew it.

He enjoyed his job, aspiring only to do his assignment well and with integrity. I remember being very upset and angry to learn that younger men at C&T were being promoted over him, men who had learned the trade under my father's tutelage. At 15, without my father knowing and with the boldness of a fifteen-year-old, I wrote and sent an angry letter to my dad's bosses, letting them know what I thought about this situation of passing over my father for a promotion to a supervisory position. From my view, it was not right—he worked hard and deserved such; however, from his "eye," his choice. Let me explain. I did not get a response from the company that I recall, but nearly 30 years later, when I saw Mr. Callis at my father's funeral, in

1994, I asked him about the letter. He said they offered my dad advanced supervisory positions on several occasions, but "Jim" did not want them. A young girl's anger released and the longtime disrespect for a company turned into an overwhelming respect and a confirming life lesson (**the worth of the "full story" before we act**)—all in that moment. I know my dad noticed the initial oversight; he never grieved over it just like he did not in the situation of "losing an eye." My dad simply loved what he did as a mechanic for Callis and Thompson. He valued what was his gift to contribute to the company and they did value him.

Returning home each night from work at 5:30 P.M., the dining room table was set, and dinner was ready without fail.

He was a "comforter and gentle counsel."

> *"I remember running away from trouble to Grandpop's 'TV room' to sit in his recliner…and the 'grenade juice.'"*

(manufactured name: Little Hug)
[Gala, Granddaughter]

> *"Now Pop-Pop, my gentle soul. I would crawl up in his chair with him in his den with my pacifier and watch TV till we fall asleep together. He might even give me a little snack from time to time."*

[Gia, Granddaughter]

In 1969, I was a student at Clark University, located in Worcester, Massachusetts. The black student union took over the administration building of the University. Protests were a phenomenon of this time in the context of the Vietnam War, Grant Park and the Chicago Democrat National Committee convention; assassinations of Martin Luther King, Malcolm X and Robert Kennedy Jr.; chaos and unrest. There was a total of seven black students in my class cohort; about thirty in a total school enrollment of approximately four hundred.

I did not take part. I had been a part of the Deans' Administrative Office as a work study student since my freshman year. I worked daily alongside Deans Marcia Savage and Tompkin, and with Joyce and Mary, their assistants. I had a relationship with them; I liked them, and they liked me. I could not connect nor understand the disdain levied against them with this takeover. I wondered at what point would persons like Mary (a different one from above and a best friend still, to this day) or any white person be acceptable in their eyes.

I called my father. His comfort and counsel allowed me the space to be in doubt and manage through. A bigger lesson was being taught: **When in doubt or not in understanding of a situation, pause**; remove yourself until YOU have gathered more information and have **convinced yourself of the reason for your action or inaction.** You pause long enough to know what you truly believe, test the situation against that belief to assure it is not a "go along to get along" place for you. It is in that power of choice, that power of belief, that power of faith that makes your actions compelling and defendable. It can be a lonely place—but one of truth and foundational stability. In the fastness of today, I do not believe people have paused long enough to know what their core belief is nor what is truth. Most follow the popular narrative to be popular or to not be cancelled, and it is anchored in fear rather than a "rightness."

From this moment in 1969 (and many other moments with my father), I have come to manage my life with integrity and courage. I do not live in fear.

"I am able to see so far because he showed us so much."

(Rob Hubbard, co-director and producer of the documentary *Through My Father's Eye*, in reflection of my Pop's story)

He was born in 1917 into a family of fifteen children—he was the eighth; five of my grandmother's births were stillborn. World War I was in its third year and Woodrow Wilson was President. Pop started school at age six [1923] in the first grade. High school started at grade eight.

"You were lucky if you got to start school at that early an age, because most Black children had to wait until they were eight, nine and even ten. Black children had to walk two and one-half miles to the nearest school in Denton and younger children were too small to be walking that distance."

[Pop]

He could not start a year earlier because he was considered too small. His morning started at 5:30 A.M. with chores, like milking the family's two cows, before starting off for school. He would start for school about 7:30. If the school bus driver for the white students had finished delivering his load of children, then he might pick up he and his siblings if it were raining. He remembers the teachers really caring about their students and wanting and encouraging all of them to learn. When there was a disciplinary problem, his teacher, Mrs. Ward, would send the bigger boys out to get some sticks to use as switches.

"I only got whipped once. Mrs. Ward gave me a smack on the hand with a ruler."

[Pop]

"The twins, Samara and Samuel, came home with me and helped me bottle feed a 3-week-old calf. Afterwards we came around the dinner table and I started talking about your father. I told the six years old about the school bus and Samara said, 'It is not right. That was a hard life.' And Samuel said, 'Samara, that was history.' Samara proceeded to tell me what it meant for your father to milk a cow. They wanted to know if his parents knew that he was walking to school. It was such an opportunity to talk about different times in life, differences of people and that GOD loves us all and we will go to Heaven. They are seeing 'through your father's eye.'"

[Judy Goforth Parker]

[Pop's] parents expected them to behave and he remembers his mother saying, "If you're gonna get in trouble, then you'd better put on two pairs of pants because those teachers will wear you out!" She also said, "If you respect teachers, then they will respect you."

About 1984, Pop started going to the Denton town meetings, was noticed and urged to run for Town Commissioner. He won and six years later was the first Black Mayor of the town of Denton [Ibid].

In 1994, Pop passed away at the age of 76, holding a position as a Town Commissioner and former Mayor. Commissioner Lester Branson stated, "Somebody will have to fill his position, but they'll never fill his shoes. He was a fine gentleman. I will miss him personally as a friend, but I really think that the town government will miss him even more." *The Star Democrat* article written by Peter Howell continues like this: "Coursey was first elected to the town commission in 1985. He served as mayor in 1990 and he served on the Denton Planning Commission from 1976 to 1985. The consensus among those who knew and worked with 'Mr. Jim' is that he was universally admired and will be sorely missed." "He was probably one of the most widely respected people in this town," said former Mayor Larry Porter. [Just for note, Larry Porter was a high school classmate of my younger brother, Bobby.] "He didn't say much," said Mayor William Eaton, "but when he said something, it was worthwhile listening to Coursey's opinions, though seldom voiced, were widely heeded." Porter agrees that "when he said something, people listened." And he added, "Coursey never minced words. When he spoke, everybody knew exactly where he stood. Coursey is remembered as a man who saw the good in people and got things done." Demetria Johns, a person who worked in the office with my Pop, says, "He treated you like you were a friend, instead of an employee here." Although his fellow commissioners relied on him to bring the black community's concerns to their attention, Lester Branson said, "I really think that he represented all of Denton." Mrs. Frances Ricketts, a longtime friend of our family, was quoted in this article as saying of my father that "He was everybody's friend. Jimmy was a man for all people. He had friends in high places and friends in low places. It didn't matter to him. He didn't see color, he didn't see class, he didn't see religion. He just saw people."

Could these traits influence how we exist, live and commune together today?

My Pop was remembered because of the way he lived: a "man for all people." My father (and my mother too, I might add) chose not to be defined by the world nor the times. He chose to define himself and to have the strength and courage to own his reality. I chose not to define my father by his weaknesses, I chose to define him by his strengths—not to ignore the weaknesses, but to pull the best from him for setting my course. I chose to learn from the greater things and leave the not-so-great ones behind. I learned and continue to learn my lessons well. Not only did I make the choices I made over time, I own them. I live them. My core is set.

Victor Frankl, in his book *Man's Search for Meaning*, makes this statement: "He who has a why to live can bear with any how." My "why" is established, and therefore, my living is navigable.

The same is available for you! For GOD designed us great... we just fail to live into that greatness!

Have you paused long enough to establish your core beliefs?

What is the foundational bases for those beliefs?

When you speak, what do your words mean? Are you clear? Is anyone even listening?

Do you own the choices you make?

["…Why do I remember Coors beer cans and 13?… I know for sure Kristen got one too."

[Tara, Granddaughter]

[As an aside: Daddy would save dimes in empty beer cans. (I suspect that is why I treasure, save and have an affinity for that little coin to this day). At one point he started giving a beer can filled to the brim with dimes to his grandchildren on their 13th or 16th birthday. (a pretty good chunk of money) After his death, Mom endeavored to continue this gesture. My daughter, Kristen, was the last to receive this unexpected treat from a grandparent and still has her can intact today.]

THE DINING ROOM TABLE.

Life happened around the dining room table

This table hosted many neighbors, friends and family members. It was the focal point of our home for casual chats or formal affairs. Several homes in Denton had "the dining room table." (My Uncle Eddie and Aunt Anna, who lived next door, did. Mr. Smitty and Ms. Libby; Aunt Vi; Mr. and Mrs. Ricketts; the Truxons; Miss Ida Mae; Ms. Violeice and Mr. Buddy, Ms. Anna Brown, Ms. Sara Ringgold.) The dining room table was a symbol of life and living. In recollection, was there a home which did not have a dining room table?

From my dad's left at the table, my younger brother, Bobby (James Jr.) sat, and then my youngest brother, John. My oldest brother, Stephen, was seated at the opposite head followed by me to his left; my sister, Gale, and then my mom (seated to the right of my father). I do not know who established the order—we always sat in that arrangement. A guest would be added first to the side of my younger brothers; if more than one guest would find their way to our table, a card table would be added to the room. The conversations went from Mom and Dad talking about things, to correcting an ugly eating behavior, to talking about our activities—sports, school, piano; to town business/gossip. The dining room table was such a symbol of family connectedness.

My father always said the Grace—the same one I say before meals to this day: "LORD, we thank you for this food that we are about to receive. Nourishing and strengthen our bodies, CHRIST our Redeemer's sake, Amen."

Mom cooked every night. If you wanted to eat, you ate what was placed on the table. Mom reminded us often that this "is not a restaurant." "You'd eat this (the food on your plate) before it eats you," she'd say (none of us had enough stubbornness to get to the point where our food ate us, though). We were thrilled when she would have pancakes for dinner. We believed it was a special national day from her purposeful announcement: "It's pancake day!" I know now, as a mother, pancakes at night is that time when you do not know what to have for dinner, you simply announce, "It's 'pancake day,'" and fix pancakes for dinner to everyone's delight. (smiles).

The children set the table, cleaned the table and did the dishes after dinner. My mother reminded anyone who was curious as to whether we had a dishwasher that she had five of them.

Immediately after these chores were finished, the dining room table became the studying/homework table. Dad having changed his clothes and departed for the Beer Garden.

I learned to play the card game, pinochle around the dining room table ("rubbing the heads" of many—including my father's and Uncle Eddie's—his brother—who both prided themselves on their superior knowing of the game that this could not happen to them. What joy when I did it *the first time!*)

I learned how to sew at this dining room table facilitating my dresses being featured in the high school's Home Economics department window when I was thirteen years of age. My first entrepreneurial adventure stemmed from this table: a *Dress Maker for Dolls* (age 8).

My manners and hosting skills were refined at this table…[where elbows were to be, souping noises and belching no-nos, mouth open and mouth closures, my head upright or down on the dining room table, reaching across versus passing food down the row, responses to various facial expressions—from pouting to rolling of the eyes;

consequences of falling asleep; what utensil to use and the placement of it after its use; what happens when you had to sneeze or cough; the importance of wiping your mouth with a napkin; the importance of "eating all your food" (smiles); talking order and respectability: "please and thank-you"; how and when to say, "I'm sorry"; what happens when you just had to vomit; and even how to dispose of that awful liver without getting caught]. Lessons of tolerance and intolerance were learned at this table as siblings being siblings had to learn to get along.

> *"My grandma was a stickler for cleaning your plate even though she knew I despised 'liver and onions'…. ugh!!!! Her famous words: 'You'll eat it before it eats you!' (In swoops, Grandpa for the rescue, slides liver off my plate and onto his. He saved me so many times!!! (LOL) I was blessed to spend a lot of my time with these amazing folks. I loved my grandparents."*

[Tammy, Granddaughter]

Where is your table today?

Can you be at my table?

Can I be at yours?

What is the symbol of a family's growth, living and connection today? Where is the place where you learn the social tenets of communing?

What is the replacement for "the dining room table"?

A dinner app, perhaps?

Or….

Is the symbol to be lost forever?

THE PORCH.

"All of Denton would hang around the porch."
[Tara, Granddaughter]

The front porch was an important place. Our house was on the corner of Fifth and Lincoln—the heart of our part of Denton. If you were on the porch, you had to wave at everyone who came through the corner, in a car or walking. It was just protocol. While we tired of being on the porch and having to wave and say hello at or to every passerby, it was such a focal point of community connectedness from my lens now, looking back these seventy years later. You knew who was entering in and going from the community—a watchfulness which lent itself to community protection in a simple way. We had a "community watch" long before it was a new initiative and a clever sign in the front yards starting in the 1980s.

The front porch was a venue for "gathering." Everybody in the town had a porch. Some were screened; many were opened. I remember many people (white and black) visiting with my father on our porch and learned later, many came to seek his counsel.

> *"One aspect of the movie that I found interesting is how the 'front porch' was described as a community breeder. The idea that sitting on a front porch and simply seeing and greeting those around you built a sense of community in itself."*

[Ruthy Mamo, '22, first-year medical student and viewer of the documentary]

<u>From conversations I am sure happened on the "porch,"</u> Pop was able to obtain funding from the bank to become proprietor of the "White Swan" (located on the northern corner of 5th and High streets and affectionately known to everyone as the "Beer Garden") in 1954. The cost to take over the business vacated by the previous owner was $4200. He needed twenty community signatures for the $50 beer/alcohol license. He had no trouble getting those signatures, which had to have come from Black and White community members.

<u>From conversations I am sure happened on the "porch,"</u> Pop was an elected town commissioner and ultimately the first black mayor of Denton, Maryland, in 1990. My father was known for his decency, fairness, trustworthiness and caring, not for his color or race. He was not looked at with bias and would not look at a situation or a person with bias. His quiet fight was fortified with patience, truth, **humility and the seeking of understanding.** He welcomed conversations of all sorts, practicing "diversity and inclusion" before it became such a deliberate act and industry of today. What fantastic principles to observe as a child!

<u>From conversations I am sure happened on the "porch,"</u> the images of segregation crept in. My dad, in a high school project interview with my daughter, Dorian, in 1991, which she titled *Humble Beginnings*, stated: "…everything was so segregated that black people were blamed for things they did not do." He referred to a particular murder case—the Sally Dean Case—where the murder of Sally Dean was blamed on his uncle. According to the story we had been told, the real murderer, Wish Shepherd, was eventually brought to justice and hung on the courthouse lawn. I do believe the above version about his uncle was told to my father. The historical time could see a hunt for a "colored" man. I do not know the uncle's name, but I am told by a paternal aunt that hearing that he was a suspect the uncle ran away to the New York area (she did not know the name of the uncle; but then again, she was the youngest of eleven children).

The actual historical account, given below, shows two separate incidences [the Murder of Sallie Dean and the Tale of Wish Shepard] that ended up somewhat twisted in the transmitted narrative of the Coursey generations:

> *Marshall E. Price, a 23-year-old married man, was actually hung from a tree behind the courthouse for the murder of 13-year-old Sallie Dean of Harmony. Grant Corkran, a neighbor of Marshall Price, was implicated and later cleared by Price, who confessed. Wish Shepherd, a young black man, was arrested and hung "from gallows erected on a slight slope behind the Caroline County Jail in Denton just along the Choptank River" for raping Mildred Clark in Federalsburg, July 1915. 2*

The Freedom Riders came to Denton. [Caroline County]

The Freedom Riders were a group of people who challenged racial laws in the American South in the 1960s. In this decade, the protests were to test the 1961 Supreme Court decision (Boynton v. Virginia) that segregation of interstate transportation facilities, including bus terminals, was unconstitutional. The Freedom Riders travelled to the Jim Crow South and attempted to use "whites only" restrooms, lunch counters and waiting rooms. One day a bus pulled up and the Freedom Riders were in Denton, Maryland. They were housed and fed in our church hall, two doors (at 505 Lincoln) from our house (at 501 Lincoln), which was on the corner of Fifth and Lincoln streets. Our church was Union Bethel A.M.E., just past the hall, located on the next corner to the east from our corner. Our porch and my uncle's porch next door (at 503 Lincoln) were part of the "gathering spaces" before the march uptown to "sit-in." ("Uptown" was two streets north from Lincoln, on Market. You could see Market Street from our porch.) The scene is vivid in my mind's eye today.

What was to happen? As children, we had no idea. You could feel the tension of the community.

But …

From the conversations I am sure happened on the "porch," our parents knew. I watched the marching uptown from the porch. There were some forty to fifty people leaving Lincoln Street and the places on the porches. I was 11 years old. I was not a witness to the actual "sit-in" uptown at the counters of the place where the Greyhound and Trailways buses stopped (a place located at Fifth and Market—just up the street), and of the Corner Store Restaurant—located on Second and Market, a place where Blacks were not allowed to go in to sit and eat during those segregated times of the 60s. Today that same Corner Restaurant still exists and is owned by a Black man and in service to all.

Six years later, the Cambridge race riots (where the small town went up in flames: two blocks and 20 buildings) occurred, incited by activist H. Rap Brown. Cambridge, located in Dorchester County, is about 30 miles southeast of Denton. Cambridge is the southern starting point of Harriet Tubman's conduction in the Underground Railroad and its swamps are part of the Eastern Shore labyrinthine swamps policed by the notorious slave-tracker Patty Cannon and her gang. (The group was headquartered on her estate, which bordered Caroline and Dorchester Counties.)

Caroline County Schools integrated in 1967.

From the conversations I am sure happened on the "porch," the community's values were affirmed and witnessed. There were contemplative thoughts as the town's business was discussed.

From the porches of our Denton, moms and dads could watch the children play "sandlot" ball, being the rooters, the well-wishers, and the conscience of our fair play. All could see and all participated.

I recall being asked in an interview, conducted around 2013 or so, what could we do to increase community cohesiveness today? I answered without hesitation: "Porches and sandlot ball."

How can we have this again?

From the porches of our Denton, long goodbyes occurred as relatives and friends from out of town said goodbye, hugged and embraced for minutes, and watched until we could see the license plates no longer. Having guests was always a party—on the porch, in the backyard, and around the "dining room table."

Today, we gather and "hang" out on social media…not the same.

What is the new front porch?

We are substituting a cell phone camera view without the context or the care. We close one eye and then the other. We remove our porches and even look the other way. We lock the door. Then because we have not been as watchful, we wake up one day and wonder, "What happened?!"

<u>From the conversations I am sure could occur on the porch</u>, we would have seen what was happening and would know.

Rooted in the Church.

No matter what we were involved in or how late we were out on a Saturday night, you were in church on Sunday morning! Sunday School, Church Service and camp/vacation bible school were not to be missed. Our Aunt Anna, who lived next door, was the pianist—and we were the children's choir. It just took a few families and you had twenty or more children [the Courseys, 5; the Truxons, 4; the Stanfords, 3; the Riches, 7 or 9; the Fountains, 3; Holmes, 4-6 and what is that, 26-30 already? (smiles)]. You found most of the Black community in the three churches of the neighborhood on Sunday morning.

There were bible verses, Easter speeches, Easter and Christmas programs, Children's Day, Women's Day, Men's Day, Homecoming and a few other special days all wrapped up in the story of JESUS. You could not chew gum in church nor turn around when the door of the church opened to see who was coming into service after it started. Sometimes you got a giggle on and it was irrepressible to your mother's dislike. That is, irrepressible until a "bop" came across your face or a "serious" glaring look pierced it out of you. How quickly the "tickle" dried up.

Pride in dress, action, speech, manners were the order of the day. For me and my sister: your hat and gloves matched, and your shoes and bag matched. My brothers, in suits and ties or nice shirts, and

Sunday pants and Sunday shoes. Protocols, discipline and order, yes ma'am. The special church events, like Easter and Christmas, were preceded by trips to the huge store called Strawbridge and Clothier in Wilmington, Delaware (about an hour and some minutes away), to shop for everyone's special outfit. (You can imagine my mother's attitude by the time she and her five kids returned home.) Our shoes were usually bought from Lou's Bootery in Milford, Delaware. I recall the father (Mr. Lou), his two sons and daughter tending to the needs of our feet and making us feel very special.

Church was one of the key institutions of this era. It helped everyone and provided activities to the pleasure of the parents and purposefully to assure right living. Whatever the family did not do, the Church and school did. All were integral to this community fabric and all were on the same page.

Being in Church every Sunday morning does not necessarily equate to understanding the Gospel and the surrendering that must occur for *eternal life*. It is only when the foundational belief is set and the faith is earnest enough that the transformation occurs. When the transformation occurs, GOD's Grace is abundant, and your path is made righteous, whether it comes at an early age or at a later one. JOY cometh in the morning and regularly when saved!

(Funny, I cannot recall my father nor my mother actively praying, although as children, we said our nightly prayers. I recall changing my prayer from "Now I lay me down to sleep, I pray the LORD my soul to keep. If I should die before I wake, I pray the LORD my soul to take" to the prayer: "Father in heaven hear my prayer, keep me in thy loving care. Be my guide in all I do, bless all those who love me too...," because I did not want to "die before I wake.")

To GOD be the glory for my transformation. [That shunned prayer and the concept of dying take on a whole new meaning because of being transformed]. David prayed in Psalm 4:8: "I will both lay me down in peace and sleep for thou, LORD, only makest me dwell in safety." This was part of an *Evening Prayer of Trust in GOD*, and no doubt the basis of the childhood prayer I was scared to pray so long ago. THOU only makest me dwell in safety!

What is the reference point for kids today?

What is missing in the communities?

What makes up core beliefs? In individuals? In the community?

Does GOD matter?

If not GOD, what?

"[Idols], possessions, status and self-aggrandizement are some of the most popular deities today. False gods never satisfy; instead, they stir up lust for more and more." [3]

> *Exodus 20:4-6: Thou shalt not make unto thee any graven image, or any likeness of any thing that is in heaven above, or that is in the earth beneath, or that is in the water under the earth: 5) thou shalt not bow down thyself to them, nor serve them: for I the LORD thy GOD am a jealous GOD, visiting the iniquity of the fathers upon the children unto the third and fourth generation of them that hate me; 6) and showing mercy unto thousands of them that love me, and keep my commandments.*

Many believe in GOD, but do you believe GOD? In today's culture, it is not that we do not know the truth; it is that we ignore the truth... even though truth will set us free as stated in John 8:32.

Church provided roots. Without such our lives are not tethered.

> *"'Tis provable and true...the rootless are always violent: whether lost their roots in place and community, or in culture and moral habits."* [4]

Can we restore GOD's order?

COMMUNITY MOMS AND DADS

"We were all one neighborhood, just living on different streets."

[Bobby - James Jr.'s Son]

The fathers were fathers to the fatherless, and the mothers to the motherless. Whether High Street, Lincoln Street, Gay Street; 3rd, 4th or 5th streets, the same caring watchfulness existed. They kept close watch on all the kids and each other. The "Moms and Dads" had implicit and explicit roles in the disciplining, protecting and encouraging of the children of the community. They could even make requests of us as if we were their own, hollering out the window or from the porch, "Is John home? Could he run up to the post office for me?" or catching us on the street and saying, "Stephanie, I need you to go to the store and get me some bread." "Yes, ma'am!" "Moms and Dads" in the community were "Community Moms and Dads" for the community, lending themselves to helping each other and sharing.

The adults of the community held the same collective community values purposed to guide and help you. They were our teachers, our Pastors, Sunday School teachers, our coaches, our doctors, our police *(Mr. Roger Scofield became the first Black policeman about 1966)*, our school bus drivers, our store owners, our Scout leaders, our school principal, our children's choir director, our uncles/aunts, the town drunk... all living within a house or two of each other and us, the children.

There was no way to get away with anything. Everyone knew all the other families in this community. No matter where you went or what you were doing, wrongdoing got home to your parents really quick, defying the need for cellphones, text, social media, Instagram, or distance. [We had an operator telephone system until about 1964/5. When you picked up the phone, you would hear "Operator," and you would speak your number: ""Eight one, please" for the Ricketts; "two seven two" for the Beer Garden; "eight nine" for Aunt Anna and Uncle Eddie; "Long distance: Victor three three eight eight seven" for Aunt Lee and Uncle Melvin in Philadelphia; our number was "three four o".] Each adult who saw a wrongdoing would (and could) whip you or tell your folks on you, or whip you AND tell your folks on you. Mom would then whip you and if egregious enough, Dad would too.

> *"So, it truly took a village. I couldn't go anywhere within a 2-mile vicinity of 501 Lincoln Street and if I did anything Grandma would know about it before I reached the gate."*

> [Tammy, Granddaughter]

When Mrs. Alice or another would say, "I saw so and so doing such and such…," the parent would say, "Thank you, Alice." The parent would then instruct the child to come into the house and "bring me that limb off that tree." (*never happened to me, but to my brothers a time or two*). I could never reconcile crying from a whipping and Mom continuously saying, "Stop that crying or I'll give you something to cry for" (?!) There was no question about whose word ruled. **The community values supported, and even demanded, responsible and honest communication about our children**.

> *"…grab a kid by the shoulder and put on a firm hand… can change a mind, especially a young mind."*

> [John, Son]

The community as well had the elements of gossip, jealousy and envy:

> *"Oh, she's a Coursey. (What does that mean? I never wanted to be labelled. I was just like everyone else.")*

> [Gale, Daughter]

I recall being on a two-month winter break from college in 1969 and the gossip was I was pregnant and had dropped out of school as an explanation of me being home so long. It is amazing how the assumption of and perpetuation of negative untruths occur naturally in any grouping of people. Overall, however, it was wanted that you succeed, and it was wanted for each one of us. The good of it all was greater than the negative aspects.

This was an active "village," ever vigilant about raising the kids. There was a prevailing cultural norm in all homes. All parents accepted it and kids understood it. Resultantly, most times you would find us **behaving in front of the community as if we were in front of our parents**.

I do not know a place where it is hoped that the children grow up to be bad, to live poorly, or to not thrive. There are inherent truths about the values that come from communities. They are not unlike community values from anywhere Big or Small, City or Town, USA. There was a focus on the meaningful things for living life well in Denton: **GOD and Education**. We were expected to go to college or enter into the trade of your father or another; to do something!

"You learned from seeing your parents work."

[Allen Boston, Community Son]

"There is no unity [cohesiveness] in the Black family today. Maybe because of laws (that changed disciplining) and kid are not raised by a community. Some blacks don't really realize what our history is—what we really had to go through to be right here. If they knew, they would change their attitude. Would know how important Education is. How important it is to not do some of the things they do."

[Stephen, Son]

The community was our playground. There were no limits of the places a child could roam within the neighborhood. We were told and encouraged to stay out all day and be home by the time the streetlights came on. I suspect because of the trust and safety of the cultural community watch, there was no worry. OR, being out of your mother's hair for such long periods of time outweighed the risk of harm in the neighborhood. In that day long outage, we could find places where eyes were not on us, so we thought. (smiles)

Market Street split our small town into the black neighborhood and the white neighborhood. I could go to town two blocks north of our house to shop at Evergam's, the pharmacy, the Acme Food Store and Mr. Greenage's (black-owned) shoe repair shop. For 20 cents I could go to the movie theater but could only sit upstairs in the balcony – the colored section. All blacks in the county went to one school from grades K-12, and the whites were split between two high schools and several feeders in the county. Yet, I am who I am today because of the totality of this community and these times. What gave me my foundation for making the choices I made came from this town. I applied the values as a measure of my actions.

Communities have the ability to protect, to love and to give opportunity…and they should. The community holds the seed of a culture yet to be differentiated just like a stem cell for the body.

Are we mindful of a community's value and values? The strengths of our culture?

Are we knowledgeable about what it means to be in communion with each other?

Can we accept the charge to "love your neighbor as thyself"?

Are we accepting of the responsibility to pass the best onward from our experiences and from lessons learned?

> *"Somewhere along the line we dropped the ball as head of the household. We took what the generation before set up for us—as a result of so many freedoms and civil rights; and with so many ways to do things, in relaying it to our children, we did not do a good job in being parents. Some of us did, some of us didn't."*
>
> [Bobby/James Jr., Son]

Some of us did and many did not, I would say!

My son has created the neighborhood around his infant daughter. In a subdivision where everyone had their established neighborhood culture, his presence on the corner lot quickly became known…. and he was different. From a child, my son has easily conversed with and had a comfort with people, especially the more senior generation—his best friend as a child was 88 years old. In his new neighborhood, he has built the relationship with and the watchfulness for his elderly neighbors. They are "community grandmoms and grandpops" to my granddaughter. They embrace her, inquire of her, delight in her and she delights in them. My son has created community well-wishers, watchers and supporters for her. This community will help guide and protect her and holds values aligned for her to be nurtured into growing well.

Do you know your neighbor?

> *"One Meharry student stated, after the watching the documentary, 'Even though it might be awkward, at first, I can start making small changes in my personal approach to my community—to get to know my neighbors: learning their names and then using their names when I greet them which hopefully will lead to a relationship which could benefit both and the community. Community involvement is important in helping an individual thrive. I often attribute the higher rate of depression in our current American communities to the lack of community support and engagement.'"*

> [Cynthia Chude, '22]

Community "moms and dads" began to fade away in Denton in the eighties and early nineties. New morals and cultural values took a hold secondary to the deaths of the previous generations; aging; many moving out of the town and the town becoming populated by others who had not grown up in the town nor had a previous connection to it. No one could find the remaining thread of a community voice, the pulse of its vitality, a meaningful historical context nor orientation. There was no care to look nor to connect to the old by those now situated in the public housing complex built on the property where my father's tavern once stood. The center no longer existed, which tethered Market to High, and 3rd to 6th streets. It is easy to isolate into my own and you to yours, in this changing culture. Your business cannot be mine, except in a negative way, and you surely have no business in mine.

> *"As Denton changed, you would walk through the streets and I would find myself asking more and more, 'Who is that?' It is a drastic change for me, because you grew up knowing everyone and where they lived."*

[Melanie Potts Boston, Cousin]

In the early 1990s, a special crime team had to be dispersed to Denton from Baltimore. This intervention, which came about because of increasing crime and drug usage/selling, resulted in a community police center erected on the property once occupied by Truxon's store, on the corner of 5th and High streets, the opposite corner to what was my father's business. The drug industry not sparing this small town any more than it does urban communities of the larger cities or small towns in rural America.

Community values of yesterday are still laudable. They are transportable.

Why can't they be reclaimed and preserved?

Does change result in the worst because we lose connection?

I AM PRIVILEGED… AND SO ARE YOU.

My parents were strong in not letting others define who they were. They chose to raise their six children in a nurturing environment, to hold us accountable for our actions and at times those of others; and to not let the world of segregation defer our dreams. We were not a wealthy family, but thanks to my parents, I knew very little discomfort. I knew I was going to college. I did not know how nor what major I would have, nor the financing of it, but I was going to college.

I am privileged.

My parents loved us. We respected our elders and people in authority—not as a weakness, but as per order. We were free to grow, to vision, and to live as children in "joy." We were supported by a community filled with moms and dads with similar values, views and aspirations for their children and the community's children. We had no worries as children because our parents bore the burdens that they should, and were theirs, as adults, and did not lay them on us as kids. The community loved their neighbors and respected the traditions of church, teachers, law enforcement, grandmas and grandpas, appropriateness, and porches. My parents were for us and my community was for us.

My siblings and I came from a place of privilege, and our children do too.

> *"My fondest memory is our family gathering on holidays. The Coursey family stuck together. And our grandparents made sure we all knew who was your family."*

> [Stevie, Grandson]

Like segregation, the word "privilege" conjures up specific definitions and is applied in a specific way in today's narrative. My definition has nothing to do with wealth, class, race, nor a specific agenda to cause the majority race to kneel because of an intended shaming and a new power awarded my black skin. It is about the stewardship of our character, not money nor power, nor status of wealth or poverty.

Privilege. My parents granted us that benefit, advantage and favor.

To have come from Denton in segregated times and to have excelled beyond imagination, who would have thought I could define privilege for myself—not have it imposed on nor denied me.

I remember many times trying to go through a day with one eye closed to see as my father saw. What a challenge! He saw more with his one eye than most people do with their two.

> *Luke 11:34-36: The lamp of the body is the eye: therefore, when thine eye is single, thy whole body also is full of light; But when thine eye is evil; thy body also is full of darkness. Take heed therefore that the light which is in thee be not darkness.*

How privileged are we to have two eyes and my father to have had his one!

It is permissible for you to define how privileged you are and claim it **with all humility**. Often it comes from recalling the smallest of things in your life and being grateful. What I learned from my life growing up in Denton and what I am reminded of every time I watch my father's films and the interviews on the documentary *Through My Father's Eye* is quite often we let the world define who we are (the meaningless labels, the pernicious words). We let ourselves become programmed into living out those definitions as individuals, as neighborhoods and as communities. When we find ourselves so easily succumbing to the labels or allowing others to define us, we lose the essence of who GOD intended us to be. Our identity is in CHRIST and not what the world labels us with. The power of choice allows us to *reject* them—the messages from the enemy; *to remember* whose we are; to *reclaim* what we know; to *recapture* our footing; to *restore* ourselves in truth; and to *preserve* that truth with new convictions for living out our best lives...and we MUST! ...so that the next generation can live theirs.

"If there is hope in the future, there is power in the present."

[John Maxwell]

Where have you relinquished your power of choice?
I have a privileged position in GOD's Kingdom.
I am..."whiter than snow" [Ps.51:7]
I accept my privilege.
You are privileged.
Recognize yours and accept it!
Every day you are privileged to be living.

OUT OF THE PAST
WE CAN FIND OUR FUTURE.

"The film gave a new way to look at the future."

[Meharry Medical student, class '22]

"Knowledge of the past is the only foundation we have from which to peer into and try to measure the future."

[Winston Churchill][5]

My mother and father chose not to be defined by the world nor the times. They chose to define themselves and to have the courage to own their reality. I learned early that being me and upholding my values serve me best. Based on those values from where I am from and based on who I am, I manage my life with courage and integrity.

According to Max Lucado, one command appears far and above all others in the Bible and that is "Don't be afraid." One of the gifts of GOD's GRACE is courage. We have the power to define our own self any way we choose; each day gives us the chance to decide differently from yesterday—providing us the opportunity to do better. GOD puts us in situations to test how we would decide, desiring that we would choose HIM.

Be strong and of a good courage, fear not, nor be afraid of them: for the LORD thy GOD, he it is that doth go with thee; he will not fail thee, nor forsake thee.

[Deut. 31:6]

My father was not a saint. I chose to define my father by his strengths—not to ignore the weaknesses but to pull the best from him to set my course. I chose to learn the great things and leave the not so great ones behind. I chose to pull the best from my community, the best it had to offer. Not only did I make those choices, I own them. The most important thing I learned was how to apply the values of my upbringing to the choices I would make and applying them throughout happy and sad times. I knew where I could find my center whenever life's experiences threatened me, my father/my FATHER. My core was set, and I did not have to develop my values on the spot when I was confronted by the realities of the times, or situations, or decisions that had to be hurriedly made.

I am convinced that people have not paused long enough in the busyness of their lives to remember, define, recall, nor articulate—and then to embrace—their core values. Further, I am convinced that, if known but not set, people do not know how to use them in their decisions about living. When your core *is* set, living *is* navigable and choices about living are easier.

...that we henceforth be no more children, tossed to and fro, and carried about with every wind of doctrine, by the sleight of men, and cunning craftiness, whereby they lie in wait to deceive; ....

[Eph. 4:14]

"When you know what's in your core, you don't struggle to decide."[6.] Pastor Hodges reminds us in his book that "no one can name you, or rename you, no matter what; that GOD knows who you are; and that you need to know who you are too."

It is easier to resist the winds of change if your roots run deep. You have to know what you stand for before the moment comes when you're tempted to stray, e.g., offered that hit, that drink, that touch, that glimpse, that purchase, that taste, that "idol" to worship; when you are rebuked or disrespected. Settle your core convictions and rely on them as anchors when you are confronted with evil. Do not let "shame" be your name.

We have lived through a time where laws and institutions of authority were racist, where law and order of the 1950s were against me. **I was a witness**. The Japanese believe that the brokenness of an object is part of its history and should be celebrated rather than covered up. The Art of Kintsugi incorporates the damage into the beauty of the restored item. GOD does not cover up nor hide our brokenness. We reflect GOD's beauty all the more because of our brokenness. America reflects her beauty all the more because of declaring the ills of the past NO MORE! Just as my faith shines brightest in the darkness, so does America shine brightest in this darkness. As stated in a favorite song of mine from the 70s, "People Got To Be Free," by the Rascals, "Seems to me, you got to solve it individually. I'll do unto you what you do to me."

I no more want a person to look at me and see Black Lives Matter as my identity today than I wanted someone to see me as "colored" in the sixties, or "a piece of property"/Negro in the 19th century. Interestingly the nominative "colored people" has a new and *re-purposed* narrative surrounding it today. Are "people of color" and "black and brown people" the same as "colored people"? Are they regarded with the same "poor, poor dear" attitude? [And by the way, who deems themselves the authority to change my identity every decade or so? In my lifetime, I have been labelled Negro, Colored, Afro-American, Black, African American and of late, Non-Hispanic Black. I am holding at Black.] I have a name. I have always had a name!

The term "racism" evokes a major response, but does it get us to the right conclusions for this time? Is it the correct label for the issues really plaguing society today? Is it the root cause? Are we blaming those things that have already been accounted for in time and history because we are used to doing so? Is it because it is easy to do, and is a most effective excuse for our behavior today? Are only a few allowed to experience struggles and setbacks, to be killed unjustly and harmed? Like the term 'colored people' of yesterday, is 'institutional racism' of today descriptive of another but the same? There is broad social approval for deflecting blame. If Americans were angry at the right thing, they would go after political corruption and ideological power. Power tends to corrupt (and absolute power corrupts absolutely). Power is the new racism, 'poor, poor dear'.

My experiences, scholarship, readings and wanting always to "seek to understand" lead me to different conclusions then those perpetuated in the culture today by many.

We are born for the time we are in. GOD has made "everything suitable for its time," according to Ecclesiastes 3:11. People alive today (especially those born from the 1980s) were not born for the time of yesterday. Your birth order was to live today in *post-slavery times*, a time where one in four marriages are interracial and the first Black President was elected by an overwhelming majority—not just by black voters. The time of yesterday was a time of true slavery and institutional racism—a blight on this country where segregation/racism was overt and on radical display daily. For those living in this post-slavery time, your "yesterday" is yet to come. Those born for that time of true long ago accounted for the period of slavery and racism **AND** successfully fought that fight. My evidence? The Declaration of Independence, the Emancipation Proclamation, the Amendments passed from 1864-1870 and more than 600,000 people having died in that fight. Their success is recorded and written DOWN on paper. Thank GOD! It is settled. It is Law! It is America's Constitution! It is America!

Those who did NOT embrace the documents and their intent and who continued to fight another day against the *idea of America*— the ideological descendants—have adopted a different label and name to sustain (and disguise) their racism. These descendants decry the America which has denounced racism. Those who are about 65 years old and above straddle both eras: yesterday and today. They were born to the *time of implementing* the written laws that were to govern the post-slavery era. Judging yesterday by today does not change yesterday's intent, nor does it correct today's problems.

We are led to believe that the battle today is about yesterday, making it impossible for you to be present today and see the appropriate tomorrow. Looking back to find your cause today blinds us to the appropriateness in this moment. You are blinded to the correct issue at this moment and the opportunity to apply the lessons learned from yesterday to today. You are losing your right to live freely under a ruse of "equity." Equity's meaning today leads to inequity and not living free. A quick example: *The NFL just announced (August 2020) that there are only four related Black Lives Matter (BLM) topics players can exhibit on their helmets. What if a player wanted to don another "slogan" outside of the four allowed? How dictatorial and squelching of one's personal freedom of thought or expression. But you sell your soul and that right in order to play ball and make that money. You **must** kneel for the American flag or be cancelled!* This is what standing for "equity" is. Equity is active discrimination to rectify any racial disparity; equality is colorblind and equal protection under the law.

The implementation of what was set in America's documents became an individual challenge. Those individuals who were born to implement and charged to behave and adopt accordingly varied in that charge. Some embraced the intent of the documents and some maintained the resistance (becoming ideological descendants of those who wished to perpetuate slavery and institutional racism). It is unfortunate that those born for this post-slavery time are more in a resistant mindset than a pro-America one. [Consider the example of our current political division.]

America's essence and declaration still stands.

> "Everything has its time—Earthly pursuits are good in their proper place and time, but unprofitable when pursued as the chief goal."

> [Pastor John MacArthur]

Healthy societies do not destroy their history. Enemies of societies erase the history. We will forget without the reminders and the honest telling of it. And when we forget, we will repeat.

William Federer, a historian, offers two perspectives and a question. The perspectives: 1) <u>governments indeed progress over time</u>: in a cycle from concentrated power, separated power back to power concentrated; and 2) <u>a great civilization is not conquered from without until it has destroyed itself from within</u>. The question? <u>Could America be next</u>? Let me explain.

Plato's Republic describes how governments devolve in stages: **Aristocracy** (rule by the best, the most capable, most entrepreneurial) —> **Timocracy** (vain people who covet honor, public adulation and fame, use their positions for their own benefit) —> **Oligarchy** (rule by the few, a rich and poor divide develops, the [elite] struggle to maintain their [power] and become defensive) —> **Democracy** (middle class disappear, oligarchs are overthrown and the ones unaccustomed to leadership become drunken with power and yield to selfishness and vote money out of the treasury) —> **Tyranny,** from a state of chaos. Commoners having democratic freedom without moral restraint results in chaos and there is a cry for someone who will protect them.[7]

Most governments, in the more than 6000 years of governments, have been dictatorships. America was designed unique to this. The uniqueness has lasted greater than 245 years because of the Constitution and the checks and balances of the three branches of government. We began falling into chaos and those among the "commoners" cried for a new leader. But, instead of "tyranny," the new leader embraced and committed to the fortification of America **as it stands** and **as it was written**—promising to "Make America Great Again"—**for everyone.** The new leader tries to blunt the destruction and *fundamental transformation* of America to a less free state, to a tyranny. The new leader caused to come into light the true nature of those (ideological descendants) who never accepted the America written on paper. The new leader understands and regarded the true intent or root cause of the discord. Federer poses a significant question in his book: <u>Could America be next [to fall in the way of the other great empires in history</u>]? You can see that it can. The boxes to be checked off that lead to devolution have been (and are being) checked off.

Happening **from the inside** we are witness to the erosion of our education, the attack on the Church and family structure; the loss of mainstream journalism; the appointing of activist judges; the rewriting of American history; and the "peaceful revolutions." All institutions are changing despite key leaders sworn in with their hand on the Bible to **protect the Constitution.** Are these the same institutions indicted in the phrase, institutional racism?

Protesters in Chicago tore down the statue of Abraham Lincoln but did not touch the statue of Stephen Douglas. Stephen Douglas ran against Abraham Lincoln and lost to him. Stephen Douglas was for slavery and codified it in the platform of the Democratic party. His statue stands and Abraham Lincoln's came down. Without Jefferson Davis, there would be no Thomas Jefferson; without a Robert E. Lee, there would be no Ulysses S. Grant; without George Washington there would have been no victorious revolution and our becoming America (our freedom was bought and paid for at Gettysburg); without Abraham Lincoln, slaves would not have been freed; without the creation of the Republican party, slavery would have continued and expanded into the Midwest from the South.

The question of black lives mattering depends on the ideology you are following. However, according to America's written documents, black lives have mattered and do matter. The lives of Black-owned businesses that were looted and destroyed by the BLM "protestors," and the life of the Black guard, Officer Dorn, killed by a rioter in St. Louis during the "peaceful protesting" do not matter to this group, which claims that black lives matter. The record-breaking deaths of blacks in Chicago is irrelevant to the cause and do not matter. What is the explanation? The proffered agenda of BLM is not the agenda. Black Lives Matter (BLM) is just the veneer covering to get the caring and the emotion. Many people follow because of the seeming worthiness of the cause without understanding the full intent of "the movement": to defund the police, to destroy the nuclear family unit and to destroy the western world/capitalism. It is on their website and their raison d'etre.. Does this truth matter?

Institutional racism facilitates the revolutionary overthrowing of the "racist system" (considered as: 'western ways/capitalism/police/a nation under GOD/meritocracy/borders), and the elevation of family structure definitions not in the anointing of the Scriptures. Those individuals who never accepted nor embraced the documents of America have repurposed the revolution under a new title. Their tolerance has led to the intolerance. "Equity" has led and will continue to lead to "inequity." Progressive ideology will always want more—a fact inherent in the term *progressive*. Progressive liberalism, Socialism, Communism, or Marxism lead to no good end; idolatry never does. The act of tearing down monuments does not make racism go away and does not persuade me to your side.

> *"The world is not overcome by destruction.*
> *It is forgiven through reconciliation."*
> And further from this source: "*....equality of all*
> *Is radically established by God."*
>
> [Bonhoeffer][8]

Institutional racism point to these "institutions": government, higher education, media, Hollywood, the family, churches, and military/police. **America, as racist, is disputed by its documents.** But, what about the makeup of these institutions? All inundated or run by the perpetrators, sustainers, and creators of racism and are now the ideological descendants. The narrated or implied focus of institutional/systemic racism that America at is core is racist is masking the true cause of sustained or renamed racism: the democratic ideology. The democratic ideology has highjacked the so-called institutions and has a DNA which has spawned the sustaining of slavery, enacted the Jim Crow laws, was the party of the KKK, was in opposition to the laws of 1864-1870, created welfare, supports BLM and has taken over the education of our children (1619 project, e.g.). The inner cities have been governed by this ideology for decades, and even when the skin color changed in the positions of Mayor/Governor/university president/Hollywood mogul, to promote "equity" or have someone "who looked like me," the democratic ideology guided their rule.

Educational institutions have polled more than 95% of faculty with this ideology, same being said of media, big tech and Hollywood. Progressive actions have taken up socialist intent. You see the family, Christianity and police being attacked by BLM and Antifa. Perhaps "institutional racism" is the democratic ideology; perhaps it is the cause and sustainer of "systemic racism." It certainly has been a part of its DNA since its inception. It is certainly true that some did not and could not accept what was written as **America's DNA** those many, many years ago. What was written in *Prairie Fire's* [9] 180 pages of a resistance Manifesto in 1974—to bring down our federal government—stems from this Democratic DNA. Many leaders of our institutions today have evolved from this 1974 writing.

Wanting to "now" count their slaves as "people" in order to keep slavery as law was rebuked by Abraham Lincoln. He instead stated that the South could only count three-fifths. **The Three-fifths Clause** dealt only with representation and not the worth of any individual. "The Constitution had established that for every 30,000 inhabitants in a State, that State would receive one representative to Congress."[10] The South saw this as a way to strengthen slavery since slaves accounted for much of the southern population—almost half the inhabitants of South Carolina, for example, were slaves. [11] Therefore, slave owners could simply count their slaves as regular inhabitants and by so doing could greatly increase the number of their pro-slavery representatives to Congress. Slave owners were using their "property" to increase the power of Slave States in Congress. The anti-slavery leaders understood that the fewer the pro-slavery representatives to Congress, the sooner slavery could be eradicated from the Nation. If the South was going to count its "property," then the North wanted to count its "property"— sheep, cows, horses, etc. The final compromise was that only sixty percent of slaves—that is three-fifths of slaves—would be counted to calculate the number of southern representatives to Congress.[12] The Three-fifths Clause was an anti-slavery provision designed to limit the number of pro-slavery representatives in Congress. YET, we have been told that as a black person you are <u>individually</u> viewed as not having any more value than three-fifths of a person.

I recall in 2000 the Republican Congress started off their legislative session by reading the Constitution. The Black Caucus refused to participate because of the "three-fifths clause"—not embracing the full intent of the clause but playing to the narrative. Another popular narrative in the Black community: certain provisions in the 1965 Voting Rights Act must be periodically renewed by Congress and therefore a substantial cause for voting against Republicans because they would surely vote your rights away. The 15th Amendment guarantees our right to vote, not this Act. But this rumor has been an effective political tool for the Democratic Party (Power). "In the 108th Congress when Republicans proposed a permanent extension of the 1965 Voting Rights Act, it was opposed by the Congressional Black caucus—composed only of Democrats—for fear that they would lose an effective political tool against the Republicans."[13] Other truths of institutional racism steeped in the democratic ideology: KKK, zoning laws that were used to keep poor blacks from subdividing larger suburban homes; economic policies intended to stop the migration of black people from the South to the North, etc., all developed by this same party who today holds the African-American community captive.

What prompted the 13th, 14th, and 15th amendments to the Constitution? The 13th Amendment, **to abolish slavery,** was passed April 8, 1864. All 30 Republicans Senators voted in favor of it joined by 4 Democrats. In the House, 86 Republicans joined by 15 Dems, 14 unconditional unionists and 4 Union men. Voting against the 13th Amendment were 50 Democrat Congressmen in the House joined by 6 Union men.

Despite the success of the Republican Party to pass legislation to abolish slavery and create a nation of equality, Democrats in the Southern states created Jim Crow laws, segregation, (black) codes and racist vigilante organizations. Republicans responded with the 14th Amendment, enlarging the federal government's power in 1868, **to ensure civil rights for freed slaves**. When Democrats enacted racial voting restrictions in Southern States, Republicans countered again by enacting the 15th Amendment, in 1870, ensuring the **right of freed slaves to vote.** In this pre-civil rights era, "bigotry itself was part of the moral establishment; an element of propriety; as essential to common decency."[14.] Many years later, in 1964, the great filibuster of the Civil Rights Act occurred – courtesy of the Democratic party.

So, when you march or protest, who are you marching against? Who are you marching with? More importantly, what are you marching for?

Why do you believe what you do?

Who or what is shaping your thinking?

What has been your instruction re: history?

Margaret Sanger and George Bernard Shaw (yes, that George Bernard Shaw) were members of the Fabien Society, whose belief followed Marxism. The Fabien Society/Marxism called for the abolition of the family on the grounds that capitalism was a system which exploited women and children, and that "conception, previously a matter for families to figure out would then be regulated."[15] Margaret Sanger created a powerful institution, Planned Parenthood, which came to be adopted by high places within the ruling class pointing to fearful pictures of the "lower breeds" run amok with uncontrolled birth rates.

Sanger is quoted in "Apostle of Birth Control Sees Cause Gaining Here"—*The New York Times*, April 8, 1923, p. XII: "Birth control is not contraception indiscriminately and thoughtlessly practiced. It means the release and cultivation of the better racial elements in our society, and the gradual suppression, elimination and eventual extirpation of defective stocks—those human weeds which threaten the blooming of the finest flowers of American civilization." To this day her clinics cluster near black neighborhoods. Our nation has come to believe that aborting our babies is "right," "a legitimate choice," even up until after the baby is born. (Virginia Governor, Ralph Northam, Washington Radio Station (WTOP), January 30, 2019)

Root cause or root intent does not matter obviously.

Institutional racism, so loudly shouted today from every corner of our society, may better be called, in this post-slavery era, *absolute power corrupted and corrupted, absolutely*—wrapped up in basic foundational principles of Marxism. Darwin's *Origin of Species* was read and reread by Karl Marx, who saw "survival of the fittest" as validating his "dialectical conflict," where labor and community organizers would create domestic chaos to enable communist dictators to usurp power." Ms. Sanger and her ilk had the power to initiate and institutionalize the "Negro Project" in 1939. (In a report entitled "Birth Control and the Negro," Sanger and her coauthors identified blacks as the "great problem" of the South... and developed a birth-control program geared toward this population.")[16] Sanger, Shaw and Marx were all influenced by Darwinism. Patrisse Cullors, Alicia Garza, and Opal Tometi bring us Black Lives Matter from their ideology as Marxist. The popular embracing of these things further point to the blatant DNA described above. It is not America.

Where is the apology and/or cry for dismantling of this ideology whose DNA has contained racism throughout history?

My life matters, not because of my skin color, my life matters because America says so. My life matters because I am GOD's child. (Romans 8:15-17)

Nazism, Fascism and Communism taught that citizens exist for the State's benefit, whereas America's founders believed that the State existed for the citizen's benefit.[17] "Ronald Reagan commented: 'How do you tell a communist?' 'Well, it's someone who reads Marx and Lenin.' 'And how do you tell an anti-Communist?' 'It's someone who understands Marx and Lenin.'"[18]

Out of the past we find our future. Out of the past we find truth.

What from your past do you bring forth as the better?

There exists a community of well-wishers and watchers designated to speak positive words into your life, designated to assist in shifting the atmosphere around you, like the community moms and dads in my life. It only takes one! You must seek them out and, as well, become that for others. Knowing what we believe and why we believe it is foundational to our ability to be people of positive influence. Knowing history in its purity gives us hope for the future so we can preserve that which is good.

Reflect on the truths of the past to better your future.

When we fail to remember what comes out of the past, we cannot get into the future. We will repeat the wrongs; we will fail to learn from and preserve for the better.

REFLECTING ON TODAY THROUGH MY FATHER'S EYE.

I Thessalonians 5:21: Prove all things; hold fast that which is good.

I recall in the 50s and early 60s our "road" trips to Tuskegee, Alabama. My mother's oldest sister lived there. The key to the success of that trip during this decade was stopping only at Stuckey's, a chain of roadside stores along the way. My dad would emphasize that because he felt we would be less discriminated against or would not meet any obvious show of racism. Today I do not have to watch for a particular exit, place or neighborhood to stop to eat or find relief. As Shelby Steele says in his book *White Guilt*: "I can sleep or eat anywhere my wallet would take me ... searching only for a restaurant that suited me, not one that would have me."[19]

I ask in the documentary, "How would my father respond to the narrative: white cops killing blacks?" I feel the need to expound further because of the culture set upon us at this time.

My father was a thoughtful man, much aware of communism during his time and knowing it should be resisted as something evil. His political leanings were that of a Republican and I think I know why. While I do not recall much talk around the "dining room" table of politics, I recall bits and pieces: Nixon versus Kennedy, Communism, and of course there were the Freedom Riders.

It is legitimate for Blacks to ask if our lives matter when you look into the places where blacks are mostly concentrated and then at the governance ideology. It is not because of the police that black lives do not matter in these concentrated places. Poor Blacks did not benefit even from the change from a white mayor to a black one. The narrative "It would be better if there were someone looking like me" has been proven wrong. Inner-city conditions are defined by blighted neighborhoods, poor education from failing schools, housing weariness, food insecurity, homelessness, high unemployment, increasing crime, economic desert, drugs, out-of-wedlock births, fatherless homes, and more...you know the reality. The status of the inner city is deteriorating every year or at a minimum not getting better despite the promises from the politicians in charge *even those* who look like me. What all these places have in common is the ideology perpetuated since America declared "all men are created equal."

> *[An aside, how do you become "rich" as a public servant?*
> *How does a Senator whose annual salary is $174,000*
> *become a millionaire?] We should wonder about that.*

The tactics today are different and yet the same in some instances: sustaining the concept of victimhood; promising everything and anything; establishing a position that the government is better at providing over your life; using fear to disguise what is actually bullying; distorting our sense of inalienable rights; distorting our authenticity—if we do not hate America or vote democratic then we are not "black"; and using identity politics as the rallying cry. This is all done with a willing populace...or race. The ideology wants and needs to hold power and "black and brown" (colored people) afford them that power; a power which dictates how you should live, work or play. They know you will vote for them and ignore your reality. They can establish a need for themselves in your lives and the result has manifested itself in these decades of power corrupted and corrupted absolutely. What results is a rule and power that is more about the power and less about "black lives."

Has the quest for power blinded the attention to the realities of our communities? It has. <u>Corrupt greed and power may have become the clear driving force of this day</u>. THIS nation put into law the abolishment of slavery. THIS nation wrote it down on legal paper for all to regard! **"We the people," over time, acted poorly on implementing and behaving with respect and accord to what was actually written.** If the "woke" culture condones dismantling, calling out and destroying those who owned, or things that touched on or represented the unforgivable period of slavery, why not call out the ideology of the democratic party which has a history of acting in opposition of what was written on America's paper? How dangerous of you in your "wokeness" to not be "woke." <u>Corrupt greed and power may have become the clear driving force of this day</u>. Issues of their true essence is deflected onto us as institutional racism, and away from what is their own true intent trying not to be unmasked. Institutional racism is a term projected into something to keep from unmasking the launcher. There is a need for ownership and atonement, but not from where the narrative today is directing it. It is not America!

Being clear about what is "ours" to deal with at this time, in this season, is most important. The root of human nature is an absolute: all men are born sinners, in sin and of Adam, the fallen; man is created in HIS image, therefore, we are equal. We know there are forces for good and forces for evil. We know that because of the Adamic nature, we easily fall and yield to idolatry and temptation. We have nothing good; we have no righteousness until we come to believe in the Gospel of Grace (I Corinthians 15:1-4); and all are invited. When we do so we are commissioned to love GOD and love our neighbor, as my father did. The moral authority is HIS. When we understand this, as believers, then we fulfill the law with the assistance of HIS HELPER. Pastor John Hagee stated in a sermon: "If you are not an eyewitness, then you are a false witness." Those who are born for this time did not witness the time of yesterday. And if history is distorted and the reporting of current events/issues is as well, then "your witness" is fraught with falseness upon which you are acting. My father was a witness…and so was I.

"White cops killing blacks" is tied up in the concept of social justice.

> *"Justice requires 'authority'—not the authority of soldier or politicians, but the authority of religious truth. NO people can enjoy a just society without some standard of judgment superior to the mood of the moment…simple popular opinion never can maintain justice."*

> [Orestes Brownson, author of *The American Republic*]

Brownson goes on:

> *"The nature of true social justice…a liberation of every man, under GOD, to do the best that is in him…the socialist would keep us all in perpetual childhood."* 20

Alex de Tocqueville knew that the "American democracy is the creation of its laws and (in still a larger degree) of its moral habits."[21] July 5, 1926, President Calvin Coolidge said: "The principles…which went into the Declaration of Independence…are found in…the sermons…of the early colonial clergy… They preached equality because they believed in the fatherhood of GOD and the brotherhood of man. They justified freedom by the text that we are all created in the Divine."[22]

America's essence is codified in the ideals of our Constitution, Declaration of Independence and the Bill of Rights. "Freedom is actualized by individuals; racial unity is politically self-defeating in freedom."[23]

Quoting from a sermon of Pastor John Hagee, Founder Cornerstone Church, San Antonio, Texas, August 2020:

> *"We are still one nation under GOD. We are still the nation endowed by our Creator with certain inalienable rights that among these are life, liberty and the pursuit of happiness. We are still the nation whose founding fathers got on their knees when they were writing the Constitution asking GOD for divine intervention in birthing the United States of America. We are still the nation where*

General George Washington knelt in the snow of Valley Forge and prayed for GOD to give him divine guidance in the military exercise. We are the nation led by Abraham Lincoln that crushed slavery. You young people today screaming you are slaves, YOU ARE FREE."

To GOD be the glory, I AM FREE! WE ARE FREE!!!

What blessings of the times will we squander in the quest for power or because its origin was associated with the "white culture"?!

What legacy of faith and politics will this generation leave for the next?

The choice is ours. By having this choice we should heed the warning delivered to citizens in 1803 by the Reverend Matthias Burnet:

> *"...Let not your children have reason to curse you for giving upon those rights and prostrating those institutions which your fathers delivered to you."24*

When asked about politics by my daughter when she interviewed my father in 1991, he said:

> *"Segregation was a big issue. When the Supreme Court finally penned the law that abolished segregation, James thought that was great. He has seen segregation come to an end and even though most places have made attempts to uphold the law **[what America has written]**, there are places today, and people, that remain racist" **[those who chose/choose not to accept]**.*

I think my father would have made the case for America...as it stands. [*one nation, under GOD, indivisible, with liberty and justice for all.*]

He would have rejected the narrative of "white cops killing black people" and that young black men should be scared...given the facts and what his eye saw.

In a letter written to my mother after my father's funeral from the Chief of Police, James W. Harmon, dated September 2, 1994, he writes: "…It was our honor and privilege to have been a part of that day. Commissioner Coursey was a friend and strong supporter of the Denton police and he will be missed."

TO REMEMBER, RECAPTURE, RECLAIM, RESTORE AND PRESERVE.

Complacency is the enemy of what once was or what could be. Not remaining vigilant or engaged results in things like: unwatched backyards or neighborhoods/communities having become havens for criminal activity; the same bathroom being used at the same time by a him or a her; or the definition of male and female relegated to "how I feel" upon awakening. Things usually happen over a period of time—a little here, a little there; and then at some point over time, we awaken to find the complexity of an issue has increased and the neighborhood or nation is dramatically changed. We get tired of being on the "porch" and waving; close one eye and then the other, substituting a phone camera's view without the context nor the caring. We then remove the porches and even look the other way, not knowing our neighbor nor seeing the need to; letting the world around us do what it does as long as it does not affect me and mine. Feelings become our truths. It is better to capitulate than to stand up to the bully hoping that because I did (capitulate), they will not come after me...but they do. When things from the inside go wrong, things on the outside go wrong.

We are quick to accept a new normal in our complacency. Too often we never saw it coming and then once recognized lack the courage to remember and challenge what now is the "way it is."

Because of community incoherence, unwatchfulness and lack of caring for each other (not sure of what we believe) somewhere along the way, sex trafficking, for example, becomes a booming industry. Traffickers find victims through social networks, home neighborhoods, clubs, bars, and schools. Children are lured through promises of protection, love, adventure, home and opportunity. Slavery. Shame on us! Opioids soar in our communities doubling and tripling deaths each year. Laws being enacted to incentivize drug usage and the marijuana industry in our inner cities. Slavery. Shame on us!

What have we lost because of diminishing direct communication; intolerance of differing opinions, being too busy to really be present at a dining room table; a lapse of values as a community, nefarious agendas playing out and it being more important to do "your own thing"?

The answer: our community, our circle of influence, a generation or two of children, a focus on the right thing. Communities have the ability to protect, love, nurture and promote community cohesiveness; and they should. When they do not, something else will fill the void as exampled above.

Suzanne Woods Fisher is a bestselling author of Amish fiction and nonfiction. Her research shows that the Amish practice of community and belonging indicates that Old Order Amish suffer far lower rates of major depression and heart disease than the general population. It is speculated that their emphasis on togetherness contributes to their emotional and physical strength. You think?

Can we remember, recapture, reclaim, restore and then preserve? YES! YES! YES! YES! And YES!

"While white supremacy and racism applied to everyone despite the presence of segregation as Steele writes, 'the values prompted by that culture of yesterday brought coherence and even greatness to this free society: personal responsibility, hard work, competition by merit, individual initiative, delayed gratification, commitment to excellence, and the honor in achievement'."[25]

Can we now have enough collective <u>American</u> authority to preserve those values? Steele says: "After *America admitted to what was worst about itself, there was not enough authority left to support what was best.*" Shame on us! (Those who were to implement and those chosen to live in this post-slavery era).

In the throes of the worst, what other story could be told which can remind us of the better? The values that came from our past to tell are the idea of America, the divine founding and creation of America, the victories and the freedoms. In the story of America's struggle is the way to recapture, reclaim and then preserve America, the better for all.

> *Behold the LAMB of GOD which takest away the sin of the world!*
>
> [John 1:29]

WHEN ALL IS SAID AND DONE.

What would I like for you to feel as a result of having read this and/or having viewed *Through My Father's Eye*? What would I like for you to know and what would I like for you to do?

What I want you to feel

I want you to feel inspired by a story of a black girl who humbly excelled—seeing far because he showed her so much in her beginnings.

I want you to feel inspired by a black man who loved where he came from and did not let "lack of education, the color of his skin, nor having only one eye" get in his way.

I want you to feel that there is a message from my story to yours.

I want you to feel hope from a story about a small town, which changed over time, but holds as an example of a small town anywhere, USA, the seed of a culture yet to be differentiated.

I want you to feel that what you remember can be recaptured, reclaimed, restored, and preserved for the generations after you.

What I want you to know

I want you to know that you can soar from where you are; the power of choice is yours and is powerful. [My father leaves a legacy of strength, joy and freedom all wrapped up in attitude! How is your attitude serving you?! My father exampled being a good father, a good provider, a good brother to his eleven siblings, a good neighbor, a good community member, a servant and a good man. His resiliency was challenged when he lost an eye, when he lost his youngest daughter at the age of one; when his business burned down; and after he himself was burned beyond recognition. He loved his community and his community loved him].

I want you to know that what is in the community is in you…and that, what is in you is in the community.

I want you to know that with a set core, life is navigable.

I want you to know The LORD JESUS CHRIST.

I want you to know that you are equipped for the time for which you were born—know your assignment for your season.

I want you to know that within the throes of the worst (Evil), you can find the better (**GOoD**).

What I want you to do
Make your world change; care sincerely and be "present"…in your time.

Stay in truth; affirm your core beliefs before you act or don't act.

Don't let anyone cancel you; don't stand in fear.

Love your neighbor as yourself.

Remember, recapture, reclaim, restore and preserve.

Always do your best and be your best, because **you never know *whose eye* is looking at you!**

> *"At the end of reading this book, all I could think of was HIS eye is on the sparrow, and I know HE watches me."*
>
> [Judy Goforth Parker]

POSTSCRIPT.

Ecclesiastes 3: King James Version (KJV)

[1] To everything there is a season, and a time to every purpose under the heaven:

[2] A time to be born, and a time to die; a time to plant, and a time to pluck up that which is planted;

[3] A time to kill, and a time to heal; a time to break down, and a time to build up;

[4] A time to weep, and a time to laugh; a time to mourn, and a time to dance;

[5] A time to cast away stones, and a time to gather stones together; a time to embrace, and a time to refrain from embracing;

[6] A time to get, and a time to lose; a time to keep, and a time to cast away;

[7] A time to rend, and a time to sew; a time to keep silence, and a time to speak;

[8] A time to love, and a time to hate; a time of war, and a time of peace.

[9] What profit hath he that worketh in that wherein he laboureth?

[10] I have seen the travail, which God hath given to the sons of men to be exercised in it.

[11] He hath made everything beautiful in his time: also, he hath set the world in their heart, so that no man can find out the work that God maketh from the beginning to the end.

[12] I know that there is no good in them, but for a man to rejoice, and to do good in his life.

[13] And also that every man should eat and drink, and enjoy the good of all his labour, it is the gift of God.

¹⁴ I know that, whatsoever God doeth, it shall be forever: nothing can be put to it, nor any thing taken from it: and God doeth it, that men should fear before him.

¹⁵ That which hath been is now; and that which is to be hath already been; and God requireth that which is past.

¹⁶ And moreover I saw under the sun the place of judgment, that wickedness was there; and the place of righteousness, that iniquity was there.

¹⁷ I said in mine heart, God shall judge the righteous and the wicked: for there is a time there for every purpose and for every work.

¹⁸ I said in mine heart concerning the estate of the sons of men, that God might manifest them, and that they might see that they themselves are beasts.

¹⁹ For that which befalleth the sons of men befalleth beasts; even one thing befalleth them: as the one dieth, so dieth the other; yea, they have all one breath; so that a man hath no preeminence above a beast: for all is vanity.

²⁰ All go unto one place; all are of the dust, and all turn to dust again.

²¹ Who knoweth the spirit of man that goeth upward, and the spirit of the beast that goeth downward to the earth?

²² Wherefore I perceive that there is nothing better, than that a man should rejoice in his own works; for that is his portion: for who shall bring him to see what shall be after him?

AMEN!!

END NOTES/BIBLIOGRAPHY

Bailey, Dorian. *Humble Beginnings: An interview with James Robert Coursey Sr.*, 1991.

Burgoyne, Mindie. *Haunted Eastern Shore: Ghostly Tales from East of the Chesapeake*, Haunted America, pp.71-81, 2009.

Young, Sarah. *JESUS Calling: Enjoying Peace in HIS Presence, Thomas Nelson, p. 202, 2004.*

Kirk, Russell. *The Roots of American Order*, ISI Books, p. 473, 2003.

Arnn, Larry P. *Churchill's Trial: Winston Churchill and the Salvation of Free Government*, Nelson Books, p. 159, 2015.

Hodges, Chris. *The Daniel Dilemma—How to Stand Firm and Love Well in a Culture of Compromise*, Nelson Books, p. 22, 2017.

Federer, William J. *Change to Chains: The 6000-Year Quest for Control*, Volume I – Rise of the Republic, Amerisearch, Inc., p. 12, p. 14, p. 66, 2011.

McKim, Donald K. *Mornings with Bonhoeffer: 100 Reflections on the Christian Life*, Abingdom Press, pp. 39-40, p. 62, 2018.

Weather Underground. *Prairie Fire: The Politics of Revolutionary Anti-Imperialism* (a political statement of the Weather Underground), Communications Company, 1974.

Barton, David. *Setting the Record Straight: American History in Black and White*, WallBuilders, pp. 11-13, 2004.

University of Virginia Library, *Historical Census Browser*, at
http://fisher.lib.virginia.edu/collections/stat/histcensus/; ibid., p. 11.

The Records of the Federal Convention of 1787, Vol 1, p. 597; Ibid., p. 13.

Ibid., p. 132.

Steele, Shelby. *White Guilt—How Blacks and Whites Together Destroyed the Promise of the Civil Rights Era*, HarperCollins Publishers, p. 28, 2006.

George Bernard Shaw. The Intelligent Woman's Guide to Socialism and Capitalism, New York: Brentano's, 1928, 408-9 via Churchill's Trial, Larry P. Arnn, Nelson Book, 2015, pp. 129-30; Wallas, "The Organization of Society: Property Under Socialism, in Fabien Essays in Socialism," 177.

Written in Box v. Planned Parenthood of Indiana and Kentucky, May 28, 2019.

Op. cit., Federer, p .60.

Ibid, p. 65.

Op. cit., Steele, p. 9.

Op. cit., Kirk, p. 462, p. 466.

Ibid, p. 471.

Faith in History, TCT TV, William Federer; *Foundations of the Republic—Speeches and Addresses*, New York, Charles Schribner's Sons, 1926, p. 205.

Op. cit., Steele, p. 26.

Burnet, Matthias. *An Election Sermon*, preached at Hartford on the day of the Anniversary Election, May 12, 1803. Hartford: Hudson & Goodwin, 1803, pp. 26.27.; Barton, David. *Setting the Record Straight; American History in Black and White*, p. 137.

Op. cit., Steele, p. 110.

CPSIA information can be obtained
at www.ICGtesting.com
Printed in the USA
JSHW042358251021
19854JS00001B/40

9 781637 641286